Tramp

poems by

Brad Shurmantine

Finishing Line Press
Georgetown, Kentucky

Tramp

Copyright © 2023 by Brad Shurmantine
ISBN 979-8-89990-033-4 First Edition
All rights reserved under International and Pan-American Copyright Conventions. No part of this book may be reproduced in any manner whatsoever without written permission from the publisher, except in the case of brief quotations embodied in critical articles and reviews.

Publisher: Leah Huete de Maines
Editor: Christen Kincaid
Cover Art: *Bird Wandering Off* (Painting by Paul Klee in Public Domain)
Author Photo: Alea Shurmantine
Cover Design: Elizabeth Maines McCleavy

Order online: www.finishinglinepress.com
           also available on amazon.com

Author inquiries and mail orders:
Finishing Line Press
PO Box 1626
Georgetown, Kentucky 40324
USA

Contents

I
99th Percentile 1
Your Test Results.. 2
Lament 4
The Last Time I Taught Huck Finn................................. 5
To the Student Who Egged My Classroom 6
Speeches I Never Gave.. 7
I Was Right... 8
How He Left 9

II
Father Gooney 13
Wolf Legacy.. 15
Sparrow Hawk.. 17
Some More Birds 18
Ode to LBJs 20
Gophers 21
Shades of Brown 23
The NASA Scientist at Muir Trail Ranch 24

III
Last Birthday Card... 27
My Father and Me.. 28
Two Tornadoes 29
The Great Mother 31
My Wife, Who Doesn't Like Poetry 32
Conversation.. 33
Inheritance... 34
Forbidden Planet.. 35
Unsafe Driver... 36
Confidence 38
What Kind of Silence 39
Underdoggy.. 40
Watching Football in the Hospital 41

IV
Great Blue 47
The Dalai Lama Kills a Spider 48
Beggars 50
Weeding 51
Mother of Thorns 53
Peace on Earth 55
God of String 56
Without Guilt 57

V
Head of the Metolius 61
Sad Bastard 62
Romantic 63
December Red 65
Sleepwalker 66
New Voices 68
Ode to Tramp 69
My Ars Poetica 70

Acknowledgments 71

*Mary, Kara, Alea, Lila.
Everything good.*

I

99th Percentile

I was the best reader in class,
the one the nuns called on
when they needed to crank through a text.
That skill alone made the whole school thing
joyful, propelled my stunning success
on standardized tests.
I loved those damn tests:
the serious pageantry of passing out
sharp pencils, breaking the cellophane,
smelling the fresh cool booklets.
Time Start/Time Stop.
Questions that had answers.
I was good at that shit,
99th percentile good.
Getting those scores each year
confirmed who I knew I was:
smarter & better than everyone else.
I walked among my classmates like a young prince,
could not share their vague pleasures,
take much interest in their pedestrian achievements,
a one-boy parade down a blind alley.
Of course, none of those kids liked me.
I thought it was envy, but they
just didn't like me. Smart kids.

Your Test Results

Dear student,
Remember all those tests you took last spring?
What a bother that was, huh? But what
a nice break too, from the slur of school.
Here's how you did.

If you didn't really try, or were hungry,
or sick, or stoned, or worried
about your grandma dying,
or your parents fighting,
or your boyfriend or girlfriend cheating on you,
or all of the above, and you couldn't concentrate:
throw this report away.
It doesn't mean a thing.

But if you were in a good mood and really tried,
according to our tests
these are your three strongest skills:
Blah blah blah.
Not bad! Good for you!
But here are five skills you could work on:
Blah blah blah blah blah.

How do you work on them?
Ask your teachers! They can help you.
In fact, we sent them another report
full of numbers you'll never see
so they can help you better.

It's summer now.
We hope you're playing hard
and learning all kinds of stuff all on your own.
We hope you're often bored, just laying around,
really, really bored, drilling holes in the blue sky
with your impatient eyes—so damn bored
you finally figure out, all on your own,
what you can do. When you do,
we want you to do it!

Have a great life!
Your friends,
The Testing Service.

Lament

When you wrote *their* instead of *they're*
and were late to my class four days
in a row, when you took the bathroom pass
and didn't return for twenty minutes,
refused to take your ear buds out,
bringing class to a halt, turned in
a terrible essay, mindless crap,
five weeks late, when you plagiarized,
cheated on the vocab quiz, had sex
in the restroom stall at Prom and stopped
when I pounded on the door,
when I had to ask you three times
to take your hoodie off,
never did the assigned readings,
kept whispering and giggling instead of
working on the Thanksgiving poem
I wanted you to write, when you had
Bic lighters and a baggie of pot
in your backpack, plus a beautiful glass pipe
I confiscated and took home,
when you punched that guy
who called your girl a ho
on Facebook, wouldn't take your head
off your desk, took a shit
on the restroom floor, left garbage
on the cafeteria table, smoked
in the parking lot, gave that boy
a blowjob in the stairwell,
missed your group presentation,
when I had to ask you
to leave the room and found you
wandering the campus and you told me
your cousin had been shot,
when your dad left,
when your mom passed out,
when you couldn't care less
about anything I taught,
I should have been more kind.

The Last Time I Taught *Huck Finn*

I grew up white as snow
in the burbs of KC.
Four or five black guys
were prep school classmates.
I wanted to like them,
did like them—wanted them
to feel included.
They were not included.

The last time I taught *Huck Finn,*
in snow white Napa,
a black student sat in the room.
I told her she didn't have to read it.
She read Hurston instead,
but stayed for our discussions.
As usual, most kids didn't read,
couldn't care less; as usual,
my job to make sense of the book,
make the whole charade respectable.
Everything I said I said for her ears:
Jim was a caricature, no "hero;"
Twain got too much credit for being close,
more hand grenade than horseshoe,
exploding white guilt, not black stereotype.
She kept quiet, flew low,
the only time I ever confronted race
with a black person in the room.

Paralyzed by race my whole life,
bewildered, all I know is
I don't understand.
I want justice, I'll cede white privilege.
But I don't, can't, fathom the cost
of that black skin, or that
brown skin either. That yellow skin.
That white skin.

To the Student Who Egged My Classroom

I was never anyone's favorite teacher,
but you must have hated me.
You crept on campus one cold night
with a half dozen eggs
to send me a message.

I always loved the way the morning light
streamed into my classroom
when the sun edged over the Vaca Mountains.
That morning the light was bleary,
ugly, yolk-yellow.
Ray cleaned it up by ten,
but I got the message, Jack.

I assumed it was you because I failed you
repeatedly, and you would smirk,
refuse eye contact, refuse to understand.
But I failed others, and even my Honor students
slammed me on rateyourteacher.com.
So, plenty of suspects.

Look, I worked hard to teach you,
gave up every evening to mark your papers,
rose in the dark to ready my lessons.
I was a teacher leader, labored far from sight
to make the system work. Love fueled me.
High octane. Too rich & specialized
for your engine.

I grew kinder over time
but kept focused on the skills I taught,
would not be drawn into chatting
about my weekend, or if I had been a hippy,
or how I met my wife. Kept failing kids,
kept telling myself I didn't need
sixteen-year-old friends.
Worked for respect, not love.

Jack. You wanted the love.

Speeches I Never Gave

The graduation speech
my students never requested.
Killer speech, on gratitude,
how their beat-up Hondas
glitter and roar
greater than Pharaoh's chariots:
the history they've inherited.
And Mr. Rogers: *You only need
one prayer and it's three words long.
Thank you, God.*

The Best Man speech
cuz I was never a Best Man.
I know how that one goes:
opening salvoes of funny friendly shit
morphing into awed appreciation
of your buddy's great good luck.
Raise your glasses!
The clinking and grins,
the murmur of mothers.
But I never sat at that table.

Opening of school speech
(never a principal).
Wonder and wander . . .
Work together . . .
Etcetera, etcetera.
No one pays attention to that one,
but I always wanted to be there,
at the center, moored.

No, they never teed me up,
so I wrapped up my speeches like bonbons
and tossed them down my deep dark hold,
crammed with waste headed for China,
tiny morsels buried in
the useless crap that sinks with me
when I hit the rocks and go down.
All the things I meant to say.

I Was Right

On my knees in moist dirt,
planting Hot Lips salvia,
I once again conclude
I was right about this
or that struggle, years ago,
in this or that school,
battles I always lost.
The bees will love these little
firecracker flowers so close
to home; they'll soften
and enliven the gray rocks,
the white granite bowl
and *ishidoro* I will settle
amongst them. I'm breaking
a lot of rules, building
my *tsukubai*. It's what I do:
for starters, no teahouse.
Causing trouble for my hives,
inviting robber bees.
But it feels right to me—
in my mind I hear
the steady stream falling
into the small pool, gently
roiling the clear water,
lightly splashing the nearby
foliage. I imagine all those
colleagues who prevailed,
moving through their days,
secure in what they do,
those hot issues
that caused me such pain
settled and forgotten.

How He Left

Like you let a dog out.
Not your dog, not
You wanna go out?
You wanna go out, boy?
You wanna go potty?
Good boy! Good boy!
Not like that.
More like some dog
you don't really know,
someone's dog.
You're in the kitchen,
the dog is scratching
at the door. You yell
to the next room,
Hey, your dog
wants to go out.
Can I let him out?
Someone yells, *Sure!*
So you open the door.
The dog just stands there,
looks up at you,
big brown dog eyes.
You say, *Go!*
And he goes.
That's how I left.

II

Father Gooney

I

Old Father Manhard, long dead, tried to make
Latin fun. We'd chant our declensions
and in reward he'd sail into tales
of the gooney birds on Midway Island
where he was a chaplain during the War.
Father Gooney: he'd feed us stories
of their goofy dance,
their clumsy antic landings.

"Comic creatures. We'd die laughing
as they bumbled into flight, especially the chicks.
They mate for life, they live forever."

The Laysan Albatross.
Midway's 400,000 nesting pairs,
70 percent of the world's population

"They fly for hours without flapping their wings.
Our Creator gave them seven-foot wingspans.
Stand up, boys—stand up and spread your wings!"

They nested all over the runways.
The Navy tried everything to get rid of them.
Mangled in propellers, sucked into engines.
The Navy killed more than 50,000 birds
with bulldozers and flamethrowers.

"But we learned to live together, boys."

When feeding on the ocean they gulp down
thousands of plastic cigarette lighters
mistaken for squid. Cartons overflow
with stuff from albatross stomachs: plastic
pencils, spools, toy tops, hairpins, combs, lightbulbs,
even a small radio tube from the days
before transistors.

*Today they are eating the lead-based paint
off abandoned Navy buildings and dying
by the thousands.*

II

One million species face extinction
within decades. The current rate of extinction
is hundreds of times higher than the average
across the past ten million years.
15,000 studies examined by 132 governments
last week in Paris approved this analysis.
75% of land and 66% of oceans
have been significantly altered by people.
Crop and livestock operations co-op
33% of earth's surface and 75% of freshwater resources.

III

"Boys, in the evening the sky was full of them!
Lords of the air, like archangels, the clouds on fire,
and millions of gooney birds sailing lazily above.
Seraphim and Cherubim, Thrones and Dominations,
Virtues and Powers and Principalities:
soaring on their long still wings,
the red sun sinking into the sea
like God Himself come in Judgment!"

Wolf Legacy

The high school where I ended my teaching career, whose mascot was the wolf, created a "Legacy Wall" upon which students and parents could leave something behind when they graduated: an inscribed tile. Mostly the tiles were small and simply inscribed with the student's name and graduation year. But one could purchase larger tiles allowing for six lines, with up to 20 characters per line, including spaces: a new poetic form, the Legacy poem.

Wolves mate for life
In the heaven of
animals they run,
hunt, play, nuzzle
in each other's fur
Together, forever

    *

She pushes her pups
away, her long snout
shoves them into the
dazzling light. They
stumble out to sniff
and lick their world.

    *

Caribou, deer—weak
or young or strong:
make it stumble, get
teeth in its throat,
rip its lifeout—it's
why you were born.

    *

Hunted by hell-
icopters wolves have
no chance. Still,
the night is pierced
and awed by their
proud taunting howls

*

Running your fingers
through wolf fur you
get lost. No coat so
thick and warm and
deep and tough, so
soft—no better hide.

*

I've read too many
wolf books, studied
too many pictures,
traced those circles
wider, wider, wider
the wolves must hunt

*

Running, running, in
powder through brush
lungs bursting, they
run. Run and run.
Where in my dreams
am I forever running

*

I too will die out
in some bed like the
mushy snow where you
will die cold, alone
not hungry or afraid
dreaming of wolves.

Sparrow Hawk

My daughter's alert and practiced eye
spotted him atop a telephone pole.
American Kestrel. A smudge,
a little brown fist of a bird.

She surrendered her binoculars.
I studied his impudent head,
his wicked little beak,
the zebra stripes on his face,
and the waves of honey, steel, and rust
splattered with black dots
washing across his tiny form,
lordly as the lead singer of a punk band.

We watched a Red-tailed hawk
saunter into view, minding his own business,
but the kestrel launched at him at once,
a little zinging fury,
peppered him like buckshot.
Get out of here you prick!
This is my meadow!

The hawk strained to retain his dignity,
circled lazily, tried to shake
this vicious nuisance,
but the kestrel kept on him,
wheeling and darting around,
glancing off his back and head.
Move, you stupid oaf!
Get! Get! And relentlessly
he pushed that hawk
off his stage.

Some More Birds

1. Bird-watching

50 yards in 50 minutes.
Slow down.
You're missing everything.

2. Because He Could

Four black beings in crow formation
drift by, riding a light breeze.
One tucks his wings,
barrel rolls.
Show-off.

3. Heard

Solitary woodpecker
high in a redwood,
forest quiet as death,
taps out his code.
Anyone here?
I am

4. Sez Who?

Shoot all the blue jays
you want, but it's a sin
to kill a mockingbird,
says Atticus Finch.
Shoot all the Finches
you want, says blue jay.

5.   Breaking the Drought

Red-tailed hawk atop
a telephone pole,
eyes pinned to puffs of dirt
a gopher expels,
digging through dirt and gravel
dry as chalk, whose
head pokes out to sniff the air.
The hawk falls like rain.

6.   Desert Pirouette

Cacti cower in scraps of shade,
lizards press into rock,
drugged by the sun.
Saguaro flowers,
white blossoms at dawn,
are rimmed with ash.

A blur of hummingbird
whirls through the crusty heat
like a burning jewel,
sips beads of resin from
the withered buds,
and stings this bitter land,
all bristles and dust,
into dance.

Ode to LBJs

"The term 'sparrow' covers a wide range of relatively small, mostly drab brown birds, which birders often call "LBJs" or "little brown jobs" because they can be notoriously difficult to identify."

Blessed be the nameless poets,
we wee ones,
little brown jobs who chitter away
and fly into windows.
Blessed be the painters behind their easels
on the concrete pier, their parchments blue.

All the little yellow flowers on skinny stalks,
mowed down each week, who spring back up
to feed the bees: bless you.

Sons and daughters no one adores,
who eat alone, snuggle with cats,
go to bars to be seen & watch football,
who hold up little bits of their life
on Instagram: thank you.

Insects click away in the grass.
Someone knows your name, your face,
admires your barbed thighs.
Listens.

Gophers

All night it poured,
a heavy persistent rain,
and I prayed the gophers
were drowning.

When I walk my field
after rain like this,
water gushes from their holes,
but I never see any soggy
little bodies. The gophers
are down deep, cuddled up,
happy their tunnels
are cleaned out,
the ground softened,
storing up energy,
eager to break out in new
exciting directions—
like that fruit tree over there
I just planted.

There's no getting rid
of these gophers—
my two cats are worthless.
Days ago they caught one
but kept playing with it,
wouldn't finish the job.
I had to hit it with a shovel.

I have chickens, ducks, cats,
and gophers, lots of gophers.
If there was just one or two
I might even feed them.
They are like my bad habits,
my sins and weaknesses,
poking out everywhere,
perforating and taunting me.

Can I come to terms with them,
give them their place,
learn to appreciate
their lithe brown silken bodies,
perfect whiskers, sharp teeth and claws,
amazing engineering skill?
Just let them be.

Shades of Brown

Fields the color of a lion,
not one color.
Waves of dark honey roll through dead grass,
patches of sandy tan.
Tree trunks stick out, dried turds,
like the scat the little coyote left,
that tawny ghost.
Pebbles in the dry stream bed
where water rivulets down
when there was water
are camel, caramel, coffee,
chestnut and cocoa, copper, taupe,
rust and russet, mahogany and walnut,
more beautiful when they glisten wet.
What isn't more beautiful wet?
"Shades of brown can be produced
by combining red, yellow, and black pigments"
or withholding water for months or years.
Taupe is French for mole
whose rocky, russet mounds proliferate
like acne, perforate my lawn.
They dig deeper, deeper, seeking worms,
wiggles of raw umber craving moisture.
Dry leaves from my maple trees
which I can't water
because my well is dry
create a crunchy chocolate blanket
weirdly pleasing to kick through
as I patrol & count dead bushes.

The lions snooze on a savannah hillside,
shifting like sand,
their muzzles smeared
with dry blood and caked with liver.
The guides whisper warnings:
Take all the pictures you want,
but stay in the truck.
Stay in the truck.

The NASA Scientist at Muir Trail Ranch

There is infinite hope, but not for us. —Kafka

In this, the second summer of Trump's
pillage, we hike one morning
to Piute Creek and sit beneath the bridge,
eat lunch, plunge our bare feet into the roaring
crystal water, so cold
it makes our bones ache—
suspiciously cold, that senator
holding a snowball argued
if the planet is truly heating
like the eggheads claim.

At dinner we sit with an egghead
and learn:
a hundred billion stars in the Milky Way
and every star has a planet or more.
Twenty-five billion goldilocks planets,
right size and place, in our galaxy alone:
twenty-five billion orbs
that could be as green and blue as ours,
that we can't ruin.
I'm hopeful, he says.

I come here for hope, and truth,
clamber across polished granite,
lean my forehead against dying trees,
remind myself
nothing can kill this.
In a hundred million years
it will all come back.
Right size. Right place.

III

Last Birthday Card

Widowed, four children to raise alone,
your mother in a wheelchair, you didn't need
a kid like me, a smarty pants, a selfish drone,
who mocked your politics, questioned Christ and creed,
took a bottle of rum for a joyride
and totaled the family car, got caught
smoking dope—who'd shut his bedroom door and plot
to flee from all you struggled to provide.

Alone, no partner to huddle with, none,
you weathered out my stupidity,
waited til I called, and loved me, loved me.
Before you died, in your last card, tenderly
you wrote, *You are exactly the son
we always wanted.* I was sixty-one.

My Father and Me

my father is a
black and white
photograph
and two slivers
of memory

in the photo
he smiles peacefully
his thick black hair
oiled back
thick black eyebrows
behind thick
horn-rimmed glasses
poor vision
is what we share

in sliver one
he towers above me
in the kitchen
laughing as
our dog stands
on two legs
to lick him
laughter
a love of animals
is what we share

in sliver two
he's behind me
pushing me
in the swing
I'm eating raisins
from a small red
cardboard box
sailing off
into space
is what we share

Two Tornadoes

Tornadoes whirl you
up into the swirling sky.
Dorothy and Toto

        landed softly. Poor Roger
        got crushed by a freezer. It

                fell on him as he
                pedaled frightened home, his
                little legs pumping

fast as he could but not fast
enough to outrace that wind.

        My brother never
        got over losing his friend,
        never talked of that

                loss, nor the much bigger one
                six months later, when daddy

died. Tornadoes whirl,
they flatten you then send you
tumbling through the clouds

        untethered, grasping, gasping,
        Earth's solid purchase gone, gone.

                The Ruskin twister,
                May 1957,
                scraped our comfy home

off the planet. Biggest storm
in KC history, most

        damage. On the ground
        two hours, slashed a wicked scar
        70 miles long,

                              right over us. Planes spotted
                              debris, 30,000 ft.:

our debris! Canceled
checks, our bank, littered Des Moines,
blown two hundred miles.

                   Big twister! Bigger twister,
                   that December, when daddy

                              died. The May wind passed,
                              the winter wind's still whirling.
                              On a sales trip, not

buckled in, he got tossed out
when his car rammed and toppled

                   a truck, plucked right out,
                   whipped, whisked up, up and away.
                   Bye bye daddy. Bye.

                              My life shaped by his absence,
                              still caught in that vortex, I

spin around the calm
core where his spirit lingers,
ghost I cannot grasp.

                   Just what kind of man am I,
                   without his clear example?

                              One who whirls, relaxed,
                              resigned, waiting to be set
                              down in welcoming

Earth, my legs weak and wobbly,
then stumbling off to find him.

The Great Mother

my sister Lori

The Great Mother is not stern,
does not gaze coldly into your soul,
nor examine your hands
to see how dirty they are.
She knows they're dirty,
tells you to wash them before dinner,
then forgets to check if you did.
The Great Mother is soft and round,
her lap filled with children,
sons and daughters and grandchildren,
on and on. She doesn't
sort people out, she's no gate-keeper.
She has a big messy house
where all the kids hang out.
Big pots of pasta and meat sauce
simmer on the stove, big bowls of salad,
and everyone helps themselves,
sits on the rug and watches the game.
The selfish little ones, the house-wreckers,
are not frozen in fear before her—
she grabs them as they toddle by,
hugs and nuzzles them, makes them laugh
and want to be good children.

The Great Mother is not immortal.
She aches, feels the weight of life
in her sore bones. Sometimes
she gets so tired she can barely
lift her arm, wants to melt
into her chair, rest there forever.
But love keeps bubbling,
makes her pry herself up and stagger off,
to clean the kitchen and feed those big dogs
she loves, but never wanted.

My Wife, Who Doesn't Like Poetry,

is right, it's useless.
I've never blamed her
for having little interest
in my notebooks & binders.
I don't much care about
her fat health care file,
so we're basically even.
She's just not into it.
But this isn't a hobby—
it's a way of being.
No better than other ways,
not as good as some:
her way, for instance.
She lives enmeshed in others,
swamped in consideration
of their joys and sorrows,
so accessible to their feelings
she must think my way of connecting
odd, if not a bit pathetic.
What use, some grand,
well-worded "position,"
when you're always swept up,
in the mix, hotly involved
in helping and healing,
inside, warm, seated.
I press my grubby nose
against the cold glass
and gaze at her sometimes,
happy for her, my throat
clogged with regret,
then let it go,
turn and trot off
into the cold
and wild
and beautiful night.

Conversation

I'm so angry with you.
You make me shoulder the weight
of every conversation.
I just like to watch how it's made,
how the strands
mingle and tighten,
how the patterns unfold.
Even the nonsense threads,
the pointless pitter-patter,
add texture and weight,
support the sudden
shifts and turns
of welcome color,
pull things together.
You don't even make eye contact.
Sometimes I see an opening,
jump in, supply a stitch or two,
but the real seamstress
deftly resumes control,
steers the design to something
more pleasing, more agreeable,
draws everyone in.
You are so rude.
I'm not rude.
I just can't think of anything to say.
I'm pulling the beautiful blanket
you weave over my head
and snuggling in,
so safe and so warm.

Inheritance

One got my hair, her love of conversation.
My thirst to explore new cities,
her unwillingness to hurt.
The way she calls home. The way I read.

One got her hair, my excruciating self-criticism.
My eyes, my procrastination,
her love of babies, her gift with children.
Her wit, my sense of humor.

My knack for writing, her exactness,
her discipline. How I think things over.

The distance & walls I throw up.
Her kitchen-craft and cheesecake.

Our daughters. Lovely beings sprung
from our love. Our windfall, our inheritance.

Forbidden Planet

When parents say we want our kids
to be better than us,
we mean a little better, right?
Except for making money—
make tons more money,
so you can take care of us
when we can't even pee right.
But in other regards just be
a little better, OK? Don't be
so fair and fluttering
you make us feel like gnomes,
or so much sharper
you're always ten steps ahead,
clicking and pointing
faster than we can follow.
Above all, don't be so hip,
so plugged in, we feel trapped
on a forbidden planet,
a clumsy science fiction movie
with terrible clothes & dialogue,
and Prospero's magic reduced
to a fat slow Robby Robot
who can't protect us from ourselves,
from the monster hammering
on our walls. Be a little cooler,
suggest a song or two,
the latest movie,
but stop gliding around
so resplendently—
stop telling us about
your ceaseless travels
and "amazing" discoveries.
Age a little,
will you?

Unsafe Driver

I was the dad, the husband,
so I drove.

At 2 am, exhausted,
I drove us home from the airport,
you and your sister zonked out,
your mother asleep beside me.
Mindful of my grave responsibility,
I steered the van through the blackness,
the emptiness, everyone awakening
as we pulled up to our home
& stumbled off to bed.

On vacations I drove, on camping trips,
cross-country, you and Alea
nested in pillows in the backseat,
reading. Wodehouse when you were nine:
Daddy, what does ejaculate mean?
Hit the brakes! *What's the context?*
"Good God, Jeeves, Bertie ejaculated."
Accident averted.
Steady hands on the wheel,
eyes on the road,
checking the mirrors,
speed ten miles over the limit—
fast as we could go
and not get a ticket.

For thousands and thousands of miles,
for twenty years, I drove. My job,
evidence of my skill & smarts,
enduring proof of how I
manage the world.

Yesterday, so serious and adult,
you told me my driving scares you.
A whale of resentment swallowed me,
but still I admired your poise and presence,
recognized your sweet intentions.

Daughter, you're right.
I'm an unsafe driver.
I'd be locked up if people
could witness my Id when I drive,
the animal unleashed in the cab.
I'm impatient with cautious fools,
make too many lane changes,
too many ridiculous statements
with petty maneuvers,
jockey too much.
Unsafe. It's true.

You ask me to re-wire
this way of being, re-learn
how to pilot my life.
Gear down. God knows
it's the least, the most,
an old man could do.

Confidence

Saotome Sensei said, *To master Aikido
you must have confidence,*
and he flowed and swirled across the mat,
pure and potent as snowmelt,
flicked attackers away, sent them tumbling
like boulders down a creek bed.
You must have confidence,
and hearing that I knew
I would never master Aikido.
I'd show up, put the time in, practice
religiously, advance in rank, but
never master the beautiful art.

In a car confessional once,
I shared my sin with Sugawara Sensei,
sought absolution, at least advice.
I'm too small, I muttered, meaning
my body, my frame, not, this time,
all the other stuff. *Small is good.
Small is better,* he said at once,
because he had it, and would not elaborate
on something so evident.

What is confidence, why has it eluded me?
Even writing this I know deep down
I'm no poet, just a messed-up person
with a twitch to write. Are you born with it?
Does it get whittled away by a million paper cuts?
Is it something a dad instills? Is that my problem?

My girls have brains and beauty
galore—did I teach them confidence?
Do their eyes snap open each morning
like cat eyes? Do they prowl and purr
through each day, alert to every chance
to pounce and play and kill?
Or do they make each move like me—
willing to take the buzzer-beater,
knowing it won't go in.

What Kind of Silence

What kind of silence do you hear
when you putter around the kitchen,
getting ready for your day,
and I'm sitting by the window
drinking coffee, staring off?
I'd rather just stare
but I pick up a book
to set you at ease.
Perhaps you'd rather I chat,
warble like a bird, make sounds
that reassure you
I am alive
in ways that are happy and normal.
Or do you enjoy the silence,
snow falling on snow,
grateful you can concentrate
on the day ahead, ready yourself
for the challenges that await?
Daughter, how I wish I could serve you,
polish your armor, buckle your boots.
Those days are done.
You are strong now, on your own,
with a strong man beside you.
What kind of silence do you hear?
Wet snowflakes settling down,
blind slimy creatures
you wouldn't want to touch
squirming in mud,
the cold black bottom of the ocean,
huge pitted rocks drifting
eternally through space?
Pick whatever silence pleases you,
sweet girl. Pick the silence
you want to hear.

Underdoggy

Remember Underdoggy?
I'd load you into the swing
hanging from a ginkgo limb
in our little front yard,
showing you off,
swing you gently
til I got bored,
and Underdoggy appeared.
He would suddenly run
behind you, push you up,
over his head,
high as you could go,
yell *Underdoggy!*,
run through, release you,
and you would swing
tremendously, bubbling
with laughter. That's all
Underdoggy ever did,
not much of anything,
but you'd plead for more.
Do Underdoggy, daddy!
You never saw Underdoggy;
you saw a guy with glasses.
Underdoggy was some force
behind you, pushing you up
to the sky, running away
beneath you.
I left you up there,
hanging in the sky.
You never came back down.
Underdoggy's work
was done.

Watching Football in the Hospital

Might as well. My favorite teams
in championship games,
eagerly awaited
before my daughter's blood pressure
shot up like a rocket
at twenty-five weeks
and her doctors had to cut her open,
lift her baby out.
Kara's recovering in the room next door,
her baby downstairs in the NICU.
No name yet. Mom and dad
thought they had
plenty of time for that.

The Family Room is small, the chairs
industrial, but the screen is huge.
I'm a fan but watching grown men
bash into each other
for obscene amounts of money
never fails to remind me
this world's not right,
you shouldn't expect it to be.
Babies are born in taxis,
in fields where women, bent over,
harvest lettuce–and they thrive!
Some babies won't come out,
two, three weeks late.
They love it in there.
This baby's mother did daily
prenatal workouts, ate carefully,
tracked her baby's weekly growth
from acorn to grapefruit,

and here we are.
My Niners are getting mauled
but my Chiefs won and no one
expected that. Fifty/fifty.
This baby has better odds.
Eighty percent chance she'll live.

I cling to the numbers
the nurses parcel out.
Twenty percent chance she'll die.

At halftime I visit Baby.
Scrub up, mask up, glide down
the long quiet hallway
where no babies cry.
Big room for a one-pounder
alone in her glass womb,
her roommates a half-dozen machines
flashing graphs and numbers.
So much counting going on!
Count von Count would light up
like a multiparameter monitor
but this street
might spook, subdue him.

There she is!
That tiny pink package,
eyes scrunched shut, pencil arms,
legs thicker, like those fat pencils
no one actually uses,
kicking away.
Fingers and toes like beads of barley.

I do a quick Count von Count:
1, 2, 3, 4, 5, 6, 7, 8, 9! tubes,
some fine as fishline, in and out of Baby.
She's 1, 2, 3, 4, 5, 6, 7, 8, 9,
10! inches long,
weighs 1, 2, 3–well, 480 grams.
She'll be stuck here
1, 2, 3, 4, 5, 6, 7,
8, 9, 10, 11, 12! weeks.
Or longer. Can't be a Grouch
about that. It's a miracle,
preposterous as Big Bird,
what doctors do these days.

Will I ever slam American health care
again? Probably.
This world's not right.

Papa peers through the glass,
beaming out the only prayer
he allows himself. *Thank you.*
Thank you. Thank you.
Won't flatter, seek favors, ask why.
Baby's alive, bigger than my heart
and more determined.
Waves of pure will flood out from her,
wash over me.

Back to the game.
Well look here,
we tamed the Lions.
In a big hopeless hole,
fought back and won.
See, Baby? See how it's done?
Outside the glass womb
we cling to omens,
and these are good ones.
But she needs no blueprint
from some stupid game.
She's on the edge, on her own,
crawling through heavy brush,
inching forward.
Though she be but little
she is fierce.

You're no feeble rag of body
struggling for breath.
You're tough as your mother,
steady as your dad,
no back down.
You're our baby.
You are Lila.

IV

Great Blue

Were he to notice me,
Jesus might love me
like I love that heron,
who materializes
in our weedy yard
like a gray reaper,
and pokes around
hunting gophers.
I freeze, hold my breath
when he appears:
deliberate, glowing
with dark consciousness,
rigid with intent,
scissoring his body forward.
I've watched him freeze,
arrested by some
sifting bit of dirt,
then spear a gopher,
fling it in the air,
gobble it whole.
How I admire him,
how I wish for his safety
and success. Jesus might
love me like that,
were we that worthy.

The Dalai Lama Kills a Spider

Automatically, while washing up,
distracted, because he dreamed
about his mother, because the letter
from the Abbot of Ganden
disturbed him, because the spider
darted out so sudden
from behind the soap dish,
large and brown, maybe dangerous,
might bite, he brushed it
into the sink and washed it
down the drain. *Oops*, he thought.
He closed his eyes in automatic prayer.
May I enter the same vortex.
May I be washed away.

My wife kills them on sight,
grabs a kleenex & smooshes them.
Whatever she was doing
or about to do
isn't as important as this.

I sit on the toilet and watch
a big brown one in the bathtub.
He's been there all morning,
or she, clambering around
trying to escape.
How did it get there?
Did it climb out of the drain,
from some dark yucky place?
How did it get in the drain?
Who are you, spider?
Where did you come from?
He's a big one. She.

I tend to leave them alone.
They'll go somewhere.
But I've killed my share,
and that's a fact.

Good luck, buddy, I think,
and turn out the light.
Good luck to us all.

Beggars

Knowing I was wrong my custom
was to walk by and pretend
they weren't there, like everyone else.
Some people are afraid of them—
I never was, but I was
critical and suspicious.
They kept showing up.
Then Francis was asked
what should we do
and he said *Give them*
some money. Look in their eyes.
That popped my logjam.
I loaded up my wallet with fives & tens,
which takes some planning,
and resolved to do as he said.
Probably wouldn't work in Calcutta;
easy enough in Napa.
Just have to staunch that gush
of saintliness flushing through
your heart, remind yourself
you're just a beggar too.
Look in their eyes.

Weeding

The villains keep cropping up,
crowding out the virtuous plants.
Herbicides kill bees, ruin soil,
so get down on your knees and weed.

Begin with beds you've worked
countless times, where the soil is soft
and crumbly. Begin with the big fat ones
with shallow roots, like obvious
avoidable sins, vanity or gluttony,
easy to pull out and so satisfying.

Plunge your fingers in,
pinch and remove the tiniest sprigs
and all their root threads.
Most offenses like barking at your wife
are easy to forgive but grow right back.
These weeds have no names
you'd care to learn, are easy to remove,
give way to berries and vegetables
with solid and serviceable identities.
Only fanatics label the weeds.
These nuisances come out clean.

But you must also confront your pathways,
where the earth is packed down
by your heavy constant tread.
Here the stalks tear away, fill your hands
with useless leaves.
The roots stay fastened in the ground, taunt you.
Abandoned friends, your cold
indifferent heart. Grab a trowel,
a therapist–but it's hard digging them out,
so many of them, the dirt like concrete.

No one else will wander here, so
rev up the weed-whacker. Pulverize them,
rake away the tatters, pretend you don't see
all the green nubs locked in place.
Push those weeds from your mind.

As you sleep they return, conflicts
to thicken the plot, spice the stew,
eternal recurrence keeping you
forever on your knees.

Mother of Thorns

Somewhere in my crevices, deep down,
in dim valleys folded between windy crags
where rocks clatter down and echo,
a dark woman wanders silently.
She listens to the kestrels
whistle by, to the wind sifting through
the manzanita, and she waits.
Her white linen skirt and loose blouse
billow in the warm breeze.
She pauses and considers the wild bees.
She fingers the ferns,
sniffs a sprig of rosemary, and waits.

She is the Mother of Thorns and Lost Causes,
Dead Ends. She folds you in her arms
so you hesitate, fall back, don't jump,
pull the trigger. Turn to her and she'll
embrace you, brush her lips across your forehead.

A waitress calls to her: *Mother,*
I'm tired. He left, he won't come back.
I hate my body. My boy's on drugs.
The Mother of Thorns hugs her tight,
says nothing, for what is there to say,
won't let her go until forgiveness melts down,
softens the waitress heart.

George Floyd called to her as he died
and she flew to him, folded him in her wings.

Mother of The End, when nothing will change.
You drop your bags, last stop, exhausted.
Call and she comes, takes your hand,
pulls you to the ground, pillows your head
in her lap, hums a children's song.
And you recover, clamber up, toddle off.

She is there, wafting through the cypress trees in one of my forgotten groves, and she'll come if I call. If I call. If I make myself, let myself, call.

Peace on Earth

He drops heavy coins
in the cup of the Hutu
who murdered his wife.

Palestinian
mother lights one candle for
dead Jewish children.

Grizzled Trump-bot,
red hat left on the coat rack,
joins the carolers.

She forces herself
to believe the buzzing drones
are wings of angels.

Fistful of sodden
robes: the drowning refugee
pulled to safety.

God of String

It dances, enchants,
drifts softly across your face,
flicks away!
Teasing and playful.
To get your claws in it,
hold it fast,
chew it like a quivering
salty sinew: the string
is everything, is god.
And then the god of
catnip treats, driving you
crazy, crunchy and
delicious, can't chew and
swallow them fast enough.
The god of sunlight
on the floor where you
stretch and bathe,
bliss out. The god of boxes
and corners where you
curl up safe and cozy,
the god of still hot afternoons,
the god of chickens and ducks,
those odd creatures.
The god of moving water.
The god of people,
their tall and busy ways.

Without Guilt

Watching Emmy sleep
on the hot tub
(all she does,
she's never caught
one fucking mouse)
I suddenly see
it's possible
to live without guilt
and still be
perfectly loved.

If I found
a gopher head
in the shed
I'd be pleased
but I wouldn't
love her more.
It's said that's how
God's love works,
but I've gotten
mixed messages.
You're supposed to
strive for goodness,
strive—always
some hunger,
some ache in the gut.
It's struggle
causes all the grief.

The gophers always
get away.
So why hunt?
If you're loved anyway?
Exactly.

V

Head of the Metolius

It gushes from a little cave in Black Butte
but originates in the Cascades,
a hundred miles away.
Cold! Too cold to stand in.
And clear. Right out of the ground.
And these old man poems—
where do they come from,
after so much dark and silence?
They burble out free, easy,
fresh and clear to me.
Sixty-odd years of tears & sweat
roiling in the caverns of my mind,
seeping forgotten
into hidden caves and crevices.
Chilling there. And flowing out
as I tilt and head downhill,
hitting the light, sparkling there.

Sad Bastard

I like to wake early, sit in the dark,
drink coffee, take stock, burrow down.
Sink my feet in the mud of my life.
Be honest, buddy: all the good impulses,
the promise? Fizzled out, fallen short.
The loving guy who can't show love.
The sad bastard.

Gentle gray light seeps into the room
and I begin to contemplate
our stuff. Our furniture,
pictures we've hung.
The life we've assembled
emerges from the night.
So many forks in the road,
so many choices I had to make,
and here I am, whatever I am.
A sad bastard.

The morning light
laps over the hills, blushes,
wraps the trees in silver halo
and dark birds flick by.
So much to love.
Two daughters, my wife.
Get off your ass, you sad bastard.
Get moving.

The light grabs hold.
My green and glowing valley,
cradle of bright blue sky,
needs tending. Fires
will come again, Trump's
not leaving:
so much to love and fight.
Sad bastard: rise.

Romantic

She is a romantic.
She doesn't know the power of words.
She says things but doesn't mean them.
She doesn't know what she means.
She knows what she means
but not how to say it.
She doesn't know how to control
her meanings.

She says *You're beautiful*
and she means you are beautiful
in your own way, in a limited way,
befitting your age and
unremarkable appearance,
your modest, pleasant personality.
You are beautiful in that way.
But she says *You're beautiful*
and the meanings spin way out
of her control, and he thinks
that he really is beautiful.
To her.

She compliments
something he wrote,
and he says *I didn't know I was so talented,*
and she says *You are!*
Exclamation point.
And she means you have a certain talent
for saying things in a smooth way,
with unexpected jolts of humor
and sadness.
Your poems, your stories,
are nice.
But he thinks
maybe she was moved to her core.
Maybe she was caught by surprise,
transported, discovered
some shade of loss
she never felt before.
Maybe he really can write.

She is not careful with words
like he is, does not parcel them out.
She says whatever comes to mind,
and her words wing out of her,
white doves released from the cage
of her heart, where nothing
is caged for long, caged only
to be born and bred, fed,
made strong.
The door is always open
in that heart, and the words fly forth
as soon as they can fly, and they
flash in the sun and quickly disappear
into a bright blue, cloudless sky,
and she has no idea where they go,
or where they alight.

He, however, grooms
the falcons in his heart.
They bite at his hand, strain
against the bars.
Not yet, not yet, he tells them.
Maybe never.
He is no
romantic.

December Red

These gray wet days
my sluggish heart springs
at sudden flash of red.
Anna's Hummingbird,
Pyracantha berries firing out.

Hasn't been enough red
in my life, not one beret
I can remember, worn jaunty,
above dark blazing eyes,
flushed cheeks,
lips painted to match.
Never bent to kiss such lips,
always preferred my women
not plain but not painted,
natural, lips pink and moist.

Never trusted red,
thought it shallow,
cheap, deceptive.
The only red I ever wore
a wool scarf at Christmas
my mother gave me.
Bought dark cars because
red ones get tickets.

Nowadays, life blanching out,
skin sagging, I crave these
injections of red,
invent memories
of luscious ruby lips
I crush with mine.

Sleepwalker

You told me a story,
punctuated with whoops of laughter,
about another night of bar-hopping,
gallons of beer, a dozen fat spliffs,
how you rose in blackness,
drunk and dreaming,
staggered up, dizzy, wobbly,
stood beside your bed, its stale sheets
tangled round your snoring girlfriend,
stood and peed on the beer keg
used for a bedside table, peed
into the hubcap used for an ashtray,
heaped with butts and roaches
and toenail clippings, and didn't wake
until your girl, splashed with your warm piss,
shrieked.

A funny story. You chortled,
I chuckled, gave you
proper shit, but also thought,
No future with this guy.
That's when I cut you loose,
my best friend in college, my buddy Jim,
who got me through freshman year
when I had a pizza face
and my roommate hated me.
We dressed alike, flannels and jeans
pulled from thrift store bins.
You always waited for me
outside the dining hall,
rode shotgun in my Pinto
on my first odysseys
to Mardi Gras and Michigan,
a grinning, good-natured wing man
even when you got wrecked.

I loved you like guys love guys,
but you were making a sodden mess
of your life, going nowhere but down,
and I was rising, flying solo.

I did what I did, abandoned you,
and not just you. Not just you.
I'm a sleepwalker too.

New Voices

*We are especially interested
in hearing new voices:
gay black multiracial
transgender female queer*
overlooked, trampled down,
dismissed through time.
We listen for those voices.

I too want to hear new voices,
and every time a poem or story
wiggles free inside me
I think I hear something new,
but it's just the old straight white voice
I can't shake, the one that's bounced
inside my head forever, whispering
You're something! You're no good.
That angry voice, that funny voice.
This voice.

I can't blame them for tuning it out.
I keep talking, munching my dry
commonplace experiences,
and they keep hearing boring static,
routine and predictable.
Lesson learned. This is how the ones
they listen for have always felt:
ignored. It's my turn now.

Only, I hear the dog
crunching his morning kibbles,
lapping up water with his big friendly tongue,
and I think my voice can't be worse than that.
God loves the sound of a dog eating,
even a neutered old mutt like me.

Ode to Tramp

> *My favorite Disney character.*
> *Jake, the Aussie kangaroo mouse, comes in second,*
> *because he doesn't get the girl.*

Overlooked, doesn't get his due,
but he likes it that way.
Makes time something he can waste.
Loves those sunny, empty alleys
where he can whistle and stroll,
sniff around. Always something
amusing to see (a crow pecking
at a tin can), always some tasty bit:
a big plate of spaghetti!
How can life get any better?
Even-tempered, good-natured,
smart. Stays out of trouble,
easily outwits mean dogs,
lumbering dogcatchers.
Cool, watchful, a good buddy in a jam,
or when a rat needs killing.
Loves the ladies but slips away
like a whisper
first chance he gets.
A loner,
can't be pinned down or penned,
roams big fields, rolls in the grass.
This life he's been given
is all he ever wanted.
Even that Lady who finally
snags him can't change him,
though he can't believe his luck.
And even those perfect pups
crawling all over him
can't cloud his mind with worry:
they're destined for even
better things. That's tomorrow—
today, this movie's in the can.

My Ars Poetica

A short stocky friend,
a blackbelt in Taekwondo,
once told me,
I can't do
that high-flying stuff.
I kick at knees and ankles.
You take what they give you.
You take what you can get.

Acknowledgments

These poems appeared in the following magazines, sometimes in a somewhat different form, and I thank the editors for their encouragement and support:

Ariel Chart: "Beggars"
The Big Windows Review: "Head of the Metolius"
Blue Crystal Literary Magazine: "December Red"
Blue Lake Review: "Conversation"
Book of Matches: "Some More Birds"
Cacti Fur: "What Kind of Silence"
Constellate Magazine: "Gophers"
Delta Poetry Review: "Shades of Brown"
Dodging the Rain: "Without Guilt," "Romantic," "Confidence," "Ode to Tramp"
Helix Literary Magazine: "Last Birthday Card"
Jam and Sand: "The Dalai Lama Kills a Spider"
Oddball Magazine: "Lament"
One Day (2024 *Redwood Writers Poetry Anthology*): "Speeches I Never Gave"
Poetic Sun: "Ode to LBJs"
Scarlet Leaf Review: "99th Percentile," "I Was Right," "New Voices"
Third Wednesday: "The NASA Scientist at Muir Trail Ranch"

I'm grateful for friends and mentors who have sat with me and helped me shape and re-think many of the poems in this book. John Petraglia, Jim McDonald, Lenore Hirsch, Joan Osterman, Tara Guy, Amy Elizabeth Moore, Andrea Bewick, Lisa Shulman (& probably a few others): thank you for your care and interest.

Brad Shurmantine grew up and attended college in Missouri. After a brief sojourn in Italy he transplanted himself to San Francisco, and has lived in the Bay Area ever since. For thirty-six years he was a high school English teacher and administrator, and labored futilely to reform public education. He is a black belt in Aikido, an ardent backpacker, and a very amateur beekeeper. In retirement he spends his time writing, reading, napping, watching the Warriors, growing expensive vegetables from nursery six-packs, and serving seven chickens, two adorable cats, and two annually collapsing bee hives. His fiction and personal essays have appeared in *Mud Season Review, Loch Raven Review,* and *Catamaran*; his poetry in *Third Wednesday, Delta Poetry Review,* and *Blue Lake Review.* He hikes in the Sierras, travels abroad when he can, and prefers George Eliot (who he didn't discover until he was 60) to Charles Dickens, or almost anyone.

www.ingramcontent.com/pod-product-compliance
Lightning Source LLC
Chambersburg PA
CBHW030056170426
43197CB00010B/1548